MW00583709

WHY ISRAEL?

GOD'S HEART
FOR A PEOPLE,
HIS PLAN FOR
A NATION

DEREK PRINCE

WHY ISRAEL?

This edition published by Derek Prince Ministries – UK
2018

ISBN 978-1-78263-591-8
ePub 978-1-78263-604-5
Kindle 978-1-78263-605-2
PRODUCT CODE: B129

This book was compiled from the extensive archives of Derek
Prince's unpublished materials, and edited by the Derek
Prince Ministries editorial team.

Derek Prince Ministries · www.derekprince.com

Set in Arno by Raphael Freeman, Renana Typesetting

Why Israel?

"If it had not been the LORD who was on our side,"
Let Israel now say –
"If it had not been the LORD who was on our side
When men rose up against us,
Then they would have swallowed us alive,
When their wrath was kindled against us;
Then the waters would have overwhelmed us,
The stream would have swept over our soul;
Then the swollen waters
Would have swept over our soul."
Blessed be the LORD,
Who has not given us as prey to their teeth.
Our soul has escaped as a bird from the snare of
    the fowlers;
The snare is broken, and we have escaped.
Our help is in the name of the LORD,
Who made heaven and earth.

Psalm 124

Introduction

As we begin our teaching on this very important subject of *Praying for Israel*, let's start by asking a question of ourselves: On what basis are we praying for Israel? The simplest answer is that "Salvation is from the Jews (see John 4:22)." As Christians, we need to acknowledge our unfathomable debt to Israel and to always pray on the basis of that total indebtedness.

In my booklet, *Our Debt to Israel*, I make the following statements:

"Without the Jews, we would have no patriarchs, no prophets, no apostles, no Bible and no Savior! Deprived of all these, how much salvation would we have left to us? None!"

The nations of the earth owe all that is most

precious in their spiritual inheritance to the Jews. This is true of all of us – whether we be Arabs, Africans, Asians or Europeans, Russians, Americans or Chinese. We all owe a spiritual debt to the Jews that cannot be calculated.

One of the best ways we can begin to repay that debt of love is by prayer and intercession. As our awareness of Israel's place in God's plans grows, let's open the Scriptures to gain a clearer understanding of the significance of the land and the people of Israel.

To pray effectively for Israel and the Jews, we need to be informed about them. The information we need does not come from the world's perspective or from the media. It comes from God's viewpoint, which we find in the Bible.

Section 1

The People of Israel

Chapter 1

The Uniqueness of Israel

_____

There is no other nation like the nation of Israel. The Holy Scriptures make this abundantly clear.

The name Israel describes the nation descended from Abraham, Isaac, and Jacob. Remember that Jacob was renamed Israel, and from his twelve sons are derived the twelve tribes of Israel. Later on, the people of Israel were called Jews. So really, Jews and Israel today are synonymous.

In the New Testament, the name Israel occurs seventy-seven times, and these references are never, never applied to the Church. Please hear that again very clearly – the name Israel occurs seventy-seven times in the New Testament and never once is it a description of the Church. The word "Jew" occurs seventy-five times in the Old Testament and one hundred eighty-eight times in the New Testament. On the other hand, the term "Christian" occurs only three times in the New Testament. These numbers indicate the significance the Lord has placed on the people and nation of Israel.

A Unique People

I want to emphasize in this first chapter that Israel is a unique people. There is no one else like Israel. As we consider the uniqueness of Israel, let's begin by examining what is stated by David in 1 Chronicles 17 verse 21. David, praying to the Lord, says:

> "Who is like Your people Israel, the one nation on the earth whom God went to redeem for Himself as a people – to make for Yourself a name by great and awesome deeds, by driving out nations from before Your people whom You redeemed from Egypt?"

In this prayer, David is saying there is no other nation whom God set out to redeem. He portrays Israel as a nation set apart from other nations. One unchallengeable fact emerges from this text: Israel is unique. The remarkable fact is that Israel did not choose this uniqueness; God chose it. This means if we pray for them just like we pray for any other nation, we are not praying with insight or understanding. In other words, we would not be praying in line with Scripture.

Let us look at the previous verse, verse 20, which states the uniqueness of Israel. I realized for the first time in a recent study how directly verse 21 relates to the previous verse. It is important to recognize that the uniqueness of Israel springs out of the uniqueness of God. Verse 20 says:

> "O LORD, there is none like You, nor is there any God besides You, according to all that we have heard with our ears. And who is like Your people Israel, the one nation on the earth whom God went to redeem for Himself as a people."

We cannot pray effectively for Israel if we classify them with other nations. They are a unique people with a unique destiny expressing the uniqueness of their God. We cannot pray effectively if we pray a general prayer for all nations, including Israel. The facts of Scripture bear out their uniqueness.

Chapter 2

Distinct Features

In our last chapter, we discussed Israel's unique positioning. This chapter will continue the discussion of some of this nation's distinct features.

In Exodus 19:6, we see God's promise to Israel while they were gathered at the foot of Mount Sinai – before He had given them the law and the commandments. God tells Moses to inform the Israelites:

> "And you shall be to Me a kingdom of priests and a holy nation."

There is no other nation to whom God has ever spoken those words.

Messiah Came through the Jews

In Romans 9 verses 4 and 5, Paul lists a number of distinctive features which apply only to Israel and to the Jews. In speaking about his kinsmen whom he calls Israelites, Paul makes the following points:

- To whom pertain the adoption, [God adopted them as a nation, as His people]
- the glory, [that is the manifest supernatural presence of God which was with Israel as long they walked in obedience]
- the covenants, [all the covenants in the Bible are made with Israel except the ones made before Israel was a nation]
- the giving of the law, [the law was given only to Israel]
- the priestly service of God [was given only to Israel],
- and the promises; [the promises were also only given to Israel. And then Paul says,]
- of whom are the fathers [let's remember that all the patriarchs are from that lineage, from no other stock but that of Israel. And finally]

- of whom, according to the flesh, Messiah [Christ] came.

This last point is the most distinctive of all the features – it was through the Jewish people – through Israel – that Jesus Christ, the Messiah, came to the world. His coming was not through any other people than the Jews.

Salvation is of the Jews

Another distinctive feature about Israel is revealed in a most important statement about the Jewish people in John chapter 4 and verse 22. Jesus is speaking to a Samaritan woman:

> "You [Samaritans] worship what you do not know; we know what we worship, for salvation is of the Jews."

This last statement consists of just five words: "salvation is of the Jews." But they are five breathtaking words. Where did salvation come from? From the Jews. This is the startling reality: no Jews, no salvation.

I am a Gentile. But I freely declare that my whole spiritual inheritance, and every spiritual blessing I have ever enjoyed, I owe to one people – the Jewish people. As I have said, without them there are no patriarchs, no prophets, no apostles, no Bible, and no Savior. How much salvation would you or I have without those five components? None! Salvation is of the Jews. We had better remember that truth and conduct ourselves accordingly.

Chapter 3
Prophetic Confirmation

I n this third chapter, I would like to introduce another distinct feature of the Jewish people – one which reinforces the certainty that they are absolutely unique: their entire history was foretold in prophecy. That fact is not true of any other nation. The whole history of the Jewish people from Abraham onward was foretold in prophecy in the Bible.

I have listed below the sixteen stages showing the outworking of prophetic predictions concerning Israel. The first three were given to Abraham.

- Israel's enslavement in Egypt (predicted in Genesis 15:13).

- Israel's deliverance with wealth from Egypt (predicted in Genesis 15:14, where Abraham was told they would come out with many possessions. The remarkable fact is that although they had been slaves for nearly four hundred years, in one night – one period of twenty-four hours – they became wealthy with the wealth of the Egyptians).
- Their possession of the Land of Canaan (predicted to Abraham in Genesis 13:12–17).
- Their turn to idolatry in the Promised Land (predicted in Deuteronomy 28: 26, and certainly fulfilled).
- Establishment by God of a center of worship in Jerusalem (predicted in Psalm 132:13).
- The captivity of the Northern Kingdom, called Israel, by Assyria (predicted in Isaiah 7:17).
- The captivity of the Southern Kingdom, called Judah, by Babylon (predicted in Jeremiah 21:7).
- The destruction of the first temple, the one built by Solomon (predicted in detail in 1 Kings 9:8).

- The return of a small remnant from Babylon (predicted in Jeremiah 29:10).
- The destruction of the second temple, the one that stood in the days of Jesus (predicted in detail by Jesus in Matthew 24:1–2). If you visit Jerusalem today, the Jewish guides will lead you around the temple area and show you stones that are just standing on their own. Then they will say, "You see, it was predicted that every stone would be thrown down – not one stone would be left standing upon another." In many ways those Jewish guides believe more about the Bible than some Christian preachers.
- The scattering of Israel among the nations, also referred to as the Gentiles, because of their disobedience (predicted in numerous scriptures, for example Leviticus 26:33).
- The persecution and oppression of Israel among the Gentiles (predicted in Leviticus 26:38–39). That prediction has been and is continuing to be fulfilled.
- Regathering of Jewish people from all nations (predicted in many places, such as Jeremiah

33). This prophecy is being realized before our eyes. It is important for us to appreciate that its fulfillment is occurring.

Thus far, thirteen of the prophetic predictions have been fulfilled in history. I believe three more remain to be completed:

- The gathering of all nations against Jerusalem in war (predicted in Luke 21:20).
- The supernatural revelation of Messiah to His people (predicted in Zechariah 12:10).
- The coming of Messiah in glory and power to establish His Kingdom on earth (predicted in many places, including Jude 14,15).

With thirteen of the sixteen predictions fulfilled, that makes an accuracy rating at present of around eighty-one percent. With this in mind, it is fair to say we should not be regarded as crazy fanatics if we believe that the remaining three predictions will be accomplished.

Some people consider Christians to have strange beliefs. But to me – as a professional logician before I became a preacher – it is logical to believe that if a book can predict thirteen events in advance with correctness and accuracy, any other predictions such a book gives should be taken seriously.

Chapter 4
A Special Response

In this chapter, we will explore the idea that the return of Jesus requires a special response from both sections of His people – from the Church and from Israel. In other words, Jesus is not coming again until both the Church and Israel are prepared to make the appropriate response.

I will begin by saying that I don't know exactly when Jesus is coming again. It is not up to us to determine the date of His return. But in Matthew 24:3 Jesus was asked, "What will be the sign of Your coming, and of the end of the age?"

In the verses that followed this question, Jesus gave a number of signs, including several distinctive ones. However, He did not answer their question with those responses. It is not until Matthew 24:14 that Jesus provides a specific answer to their specific question about "the sign."

> And this gospel of the kingdom will be preached in all the world as a witness to all the nations, and then the end will come.

When will the end come? When the "gospel of the kingdom [has been] preached in all the world as a witness to all the nations." It is clear to see from this response how His return places the responsibility directly on the Church. We are responsible to do what is outlined as the predicate for His coming.

The Jewish Equivalent

Interestingly, Jesus also spoke a word in Matthew 23:37–39 to the Jewish people concerning His return:

> Jesus looked out over Jerusalem and said, 'O Jerusalem, Jerusalem, the one who kills the prophets and stones those who are sent to her! How often I wanted to gather your

children together, as a hen gathers her chicks under her wings, but you were not willing!' [And note that "you" is plural here.]

It is important for us to understand that the Jewish people have a collective will. Many times, God addresses them in the plural: "You [My people] were not willing!"

Let us look at how the Scripture passage continues:

'For I say to you, you shall see Me no more till you say, "Blessed is He who comes in the name of the Lord!'

In other words, Jesus is not going to come back until the heart of the Jewish people has been prepared to welcome Him. He requires a response from Christians (the Church), and from Israel.

Jesus says, in effect, "You are not going to see Me again – I am never going to force Myself upon you. I am not coming back until you are longing for Me; until you cry out for Me; until you realize who I am."

Chapter 5
What God Expects

_____

In this chapter, we will deal further with the needed response. We will address these important questions, "What is God looking for in Israel? What is He waiting for?" Along with these, we will ask a very interesting additional question: "When will God come back to Israel?"

Meekness and Humility

For our first answer to questions about the response God expects, let's look at Zephaniah chapter 3 verses 11–13. Before we explore these verses, I want to add that this passage has a message for the Church just as much as it does for Israel.

In that day you shall not be shamed for any of your deeds in which you transgress against Me; for then I will take away from your midst those who rejoice in your pride, and you shall no longer be haughty in My holy mountain.

What characteristic is God objecting to in this passage? Religious pride. Let me say that there are many reasons for people to be prideful, but religion is at the top of the list.

God says to His Jewish people, "Until you have learned not to be proud because I have chosen you; because I have placed my temple in your midst; because I have called you specially; I am not coming back."

Then the Lord says:

I will leave in your midst a meek and humble people and they shall trust in the name of the LORD. The remnant of Israel shall do no unrighteousness and speak no lies. Nor shall a deceitful tongue be found in their mouth.

What is the Lord expecting to see in Israel when He comes back? A meek and humble people. What is the Lord looking for in the Church? Exactly the same – a meek and humble people.

I have come to see that the real issue we are confronting in the Church – in America and many other nations – is pride. Are we really willing to humble ourselves before God?

This point is particularly significant because it brings us right back to the parallel between the Church with Israel. In both cases, Jesus is coming back for a meek and humble people.

The biggest problem with all religious people is pride. That is true of Jews, and it is true of Christians of all denominations. In our study in this chapter, we have learned the most important single lesson for our spiritual well-being: God is looking for humility and meekness.

In our next section, we are going to take a look at the land of Israel from a Biblical perspective.

Section 2

The Land of Israel

Chapter 6
The Land of Israel

I n the first section of this book, we dealt with the subject of the people of Israel. With this section, beginning with this chapter, I want to focus on what is possibly the most controversial topic in contemporary politics. What is that topic? God's plan for the land of Israel.

In contemporary media language, the land of Israel is often mistakenly referred to as Palestine. Let me point out that it is totally contrary to Biblical truth to call it Palestine. Palestine means the land of the Philistines. That term was never used until the Romans had conquered and destroyed the second temple. Then they used the name Palestine to assert that the Jews no longer had any claim to this region. It was a deliberately chosen, anti-Semitic word.

Biblically, the land of Israel was called the Land of Canaan before it was taken by Joshua. But in the New Testament, do you know what this nation is called? The Land of Israel.

God's Promise to Abraham

To begin our exploration of this controversial subject, let us look at what God has to say about this unique and significant land. In Genesis 17 verses 7 and 8, God appeared to Abraham. At that time, God made a covenant with him which was totally sovereign. Abraham had nothing to do with this covenant. God simply decided that this was what He was going to do. He said to Abraham:

> "And I will establish My covenant between Me and you and your descendants after you in their generations, for an everlasting covenant, to be God to you and your descendants after you. Also I give to you and your descendants after you the land in which you are a stranger, all the land of Canaan, as an everlasting possession; and I will be their God."

For me, it is absolutely clear that for everyone who believes the Bible, there is no dispute as to whom the land belongs. Whether Israel is in the land or outside of it makes no difference. According to Scripture, specifically stated in the above verse, God has given it to them as an "everlasting possession."

A Firm Commitment

There is a remarkable passage in Psalm 105, which I personally consider to be one of the most significant passages in Scripture. This psalm contains the statement of God's plan and total commitment for this land. It describes God's covenant-keeping intentions for Israel so explicitly. We begin at verse 7:

> He is the LORD our God; His judgments are in all the earth. [In other words, what God decrees applies in every part of the earth.]
>
> He remembers His covenant forever, the word which He commanded, for a thousand generations, the covenant which He made with Abraham, and confirmed it to Jacob for a statute.

In four verses of Psalm 105, the Word of God uses stronger language to describe His total commitment to this land than anywhere else in the Bible. You cannot find another passage quite like this one. Let me just list the words used: covenant, word, command, oath, statute, and everlasting covenant. Here is the pivotal question: to what is God making such a total, authoritative, unreserved commitment? My breath is taken away when I discover the answer to this question in verse 11: *"To you I will give the land of Canaan as the allotment of your inheritance."*

All those words – covenant, word, command, oath, statute, and everlasting covenant – are applied to God's giving of all the land of Canaan. The strength and clarity of God's words carry the implication that anybody who goes against that covenant would be going against God.

The Return of Israel

In Jeremiah chapter 30 beginning at verse 3, we have one of the countless passages predicting the return of the Jewish people to their inheritance in the last days.

'For behold, the days are coming,' says the LORD, 'that I will bring back from captivity My people Israel and Judah,' says the LORD. 'And I will cause them to return to the land that I gave to their fathers, and they shall possess it.'

Anyone with a moderate knowledge of the Bible knows that the land God gave to Abraham and his descendants is the land of Canaan. The name for this territory became the land of Israel – the land we call the Holy Land. God says, "When the time comes, I will bring back the descendants of Israel and Judah from their captivity to the land I gave to their fathers."

Chapter 7
God's Sovereignty

Do you believe in the sovereignty of God? I certainly do. My definition of God's sovereignty is this: God does what He wants, the way He wants, when He wants, and He asks no one's permission.

A Covenant Kept

Almost four thousand years ago, God made a covenant with Abraham. He said, "I will give this land to you and your descendants." Most people – even most Israelites – forgot about that covenant. Some people believe it was buried in the past. Yet there is One – The Lord Almighty – who has never forgotten. He says: "I am keeping My covenant."

This is an essential principle for all of us to remember: God keeps His covenants. This truth is especially important for us as Christians, because our relationship with God is based on the covenant made through the blood of Jesus. If you have been taught Replacement Theology, which says that the Church has replaced Israel as God's people, you need to ask yourself this sobering question: "If God could break His covenant with Israel, why shouldn't He break His covenant with the Church?" But here is the truth: He won't break His promises because He is not a covenant breaker. He made a covenant and He is keeping His covenant. That is good news. It is exciting!

Chapter 8
Israel and The Return of Christ

Another very important observation about the centrality of Israel to God's plan is that the return of Christ focuses specifically on the land of Israel.

Climax in Jerusalem

The last three chapters of Zechariah, 12 through 14, all relate to the period of the return of the Lord. Let's look at the beginning of those chapters, Zechariah 12:1–3:

> And the Lord says, "The burden of the Word of the LORD against Israel. Thus says the LORD who stretches out the heavens, lays

the foundation of the earth, and forms the spirit of man within him: 'Behold, I will make Jerusalem a cup of drunkenness to all the surrounding peoples, when they lay siege against Judah and Jerusalem. And it shall happen in that day that I will make Jerusalem a very heavy stone for all peoples; all who would heed it away will surely be cut in pieces, though all nations of the earth are gathered against it.'"

The above passage makes it clear that the climax of the age is not going to take place in New York, London, or Tokyo. It is going to take place in Jerusalem. That is the setting for the last act of the world's drama.

The Lord's Return

In the New Testament, when Jesus ascended into heaven from the Mount of Olives, the angels said to the disciples who stood there looking up into heaven: "This same Jesus, who was taken up from you into heaven, will so come in like manner as you saw Him go into heaven" (Acts 1:11).

Jesus went from the Mount of Olives and He will return to the Mount of Olives. He went in a cloud and He will return in a cloud. That Scripture will be fulfilled exactly.

This is the scenario for the end of the age. Here is what I want to point out to you: Everything predicted in the Bible at the last period before Jesus comes focuses on Israel, Jerusalem, the Land, and the People. In other words, if they were not in place, the return of Jesus could not take place.

Chapter 9
Preparation for His Return

One very critical question about this situation in the Middle East is, "What is the real issue behind it all?"

In this chapter, we want to find out why Israel is so pivotal. For example are you aware that approximately half the resolutions of the United Nations have been made about Israel? Can you imagine anything less appropriate or more ridiculous? There must be a reason.

Why is it that every time we open a newspaper or turn on the television, there is something about this little strip of territory called Israel? We are talking about an area that is just a drop in the bucket of the world. What is the reason for the pressure, for the opposition, for the conflict? In this chapter, we will explore the answer to those questions.

They Will Know

As mentioned earlier, Zechariah chapters 12, 13, and 14 all deal with the land of Israel at the close of this age. If you read Zechariah 12, you find the final filling in of this picture. In Zechariah 12:10, it is God speaking, and He says:

> "And I will pour out on the house of David and on the inhabitants of Jerusalem the Spirit of grace and supplication; [Notice you cannot supplicate unless God gives you the Spirit of grace. When He gives you the Spirit of grace you can respond with supplication.] then they will look on Me whom they have pierced. They will mourn for Him as one mourns for his only son, and grieve for Him as one grieves for a firstborn.

God says concerning His people, "They will look on Me whom they [the Jewish people] have pierced." It is astonishing that Jewish people read this verse without knowing what it means. It is the clearest statement anywhere in Scripture that they will crucify the Lord: "They will look on Me whom they have pierced."

Next it says, "They will mourn for Him as one mourns for his only son, and grieve for Him as one grieves for a firstborn." A revelation of Jesus is coming to His own people, the Jewish people, by the Holy Spirit. They will finally know who He really is. Then there will be mourning as has never been experienced in the history of Israel. For the first time, they will realize, "We crucified our Messiah. We rejected our God." Then it goes on:

> "In that day there shall be a great mourning in Jerusalem, like the mourning at Hadad Rimmon in the plain of Megiddo. And the land shall mourn, every family by itself: the family of the house of David..."

If we put these truths from Matthew and Zechariah together, they make it clear that before the Lord returns, certain requirements have to be established. The Jewish people have to be re-established in Jerusalem and in the land, because the Lord Jesus is not coming back until they are. Then, there will have to be a supernatural revelation of Jesus which will turn their hearts to Him.

Satan's Greatest Fear

If you were asked to guess what would be the greatest fear of Satan, the god of this age, what would you say? What do you think he fears the most? My answer to that question would be simple and direct: the return of Jesus. Why would that be so fearsome to the devil? Because until Jesus comes back, he may lose a lot of battles – but he will never lose the war. He may lose a lot of souls, but he will still be the god of this age. That status will not change until Jesus returns in person. Thus, the event the devil fears the most is the return of Jesus. If he fears that event the most, wouldn't it make sense that he would also oppose that event the most? Satan looses vehement opposition against any activity which prepares the way for Jesus to return.

As we have seen from the Scriptures, the Jewish people will have to be in Jerusalem as their city and they must be occupying the land before Jesus will come back. It is so important that we acknowledge this fact, because it is the promise behind all the uproar and all the fuss we see concerning Israel. Satan is doing everything he can to prevent this pivotal step in the scenario which will prepare the way for the return of the Lord.

Thus far, we have examined Biblical facts about the people and the land of Israel. We have also seen that the necessity for Israel being in their land before the return of Jesus gives rise to Satan's greatest fear. As a result, it is the source of much turmoil among the nations.

With that teaching as a foundation, we are now in a position to look at the right approach we can take to praying for Israel. From there, we will eventually move on to the specific areas for prayer from God's perspective concerning the people and the land of Israel.

Section 3

The Right Approach to Prayer

Chapter 10
Direction from God's Word

In considering how we can best pray for Israel, we need to recognize one important fact. The prayers that are going to be answered are those which are already supported in the Scriptures. Why is this so important? Because we need to see that to pray outside the purposes of God, or contrary to the purposes of God, would be fruitless.

We are to pray within the parameters of the Word of God. We are not to ask God to do something He has said He will not do. This is one reason we need to have a clear understanding of God's prophetic purposes for Israel. That understanding will enable us to pray effectively for them.

According to Your Word

In the New Testament, the Virgin Mary received the astonishing news that she was to be the mother of the Messiah. When the angel first gave her that message, she didn't understand it. She didn't know how it could happen, but she said, "Let it be to me according to your word."

I believe the greatest miracle ever experienced by a human being was the birth of the Messiah through a virgin. It came to pass when she said, "Be it unto me according to thy word."

You cannot pray anything higher than the revealed Word of God. One of the great functions of an intercessor is to pray into being what God has already said will happen. That is why God has set intercessors on the walls of Jerusalem.

The Role of a Secretary

The Hebrew word for an intercessor in Isaiah 62 is maskir, which means someone who reminds someone else. So, according to the Hebrew understanding, the function of an intercessor is the same as a secretary – one who reminds the boss of what is on the calendar or to do list.

As intercessors, our job is to remind God of what is on His prophetic calendar. You say to God, "Do as You have said according to Your Word." There is much more to intercession than this simple point, but this is the basis of the task. Therefore, an intercessor must be familiar with the Word of God, and must have a clear view of God's purposes and their outworking.

So this is the first important principle for the right approach to prayer. When you pray for Israel, stay within the parameters of the Word of God.

Chapter 11

Thanksgiving and Praise

As we continue to look at the right approach to prayer, the next suggestion is based on Psalm 100:4:

> Enter into His gates with thanksgiving, and into His courts with praise.

Unfortunately, many Christians are not familiar with this great fundamental principle. Our direct access into God's presence comes through the gates of thanksgiving and the courts of praise.

This principle also applies when you are praying for Israel. The most effective way to pray for Israel is to begin with thanksgiving.

God has given us an example of this principle in Jeremiah 31:7. The Lord says:

> Sing with gladness for Jacob, and shout among the chief of the nations.

How many times have you read the word shout in the Psalms? Have you ever shouted? I tell people, "I'm not a singer, I can't keep a tune. But I can shout." We have an obligation to shout. Of course, you must choose the right time and place. But don't mutter. Be clear, be bold, be as articulate as you can. Shout!

Proclaim!

Another aspect of our thanksgiving and praise is found in this same verse:

> Sing with gladness for Jacob, and shout among the chief of the nations, proclaim.

Proclamation is releasing the Word of God into a situation.

Boldly and in faith, you proclaim the Word

of God into any given situation. By doing so, you release God's supernatural power into that situation. As the Lord says in this verse from Jeremiah 31:7, "Proclaim." In other words, "Release My promises into the destiny of Israel."

Next He says, "give praise," and then "and say, O Lord, save Your people, the remnant of Israel."

Please notice that in that single verse – verse 7 of Jeremiah 31 – there are five actions the Lord has outlined for us to do: sing, shout, proclaim, praise, and then pray. Obviously for us to say, "O Lord, save Your people" is a prayer.

Those are the five responses we can make to the promises of God. Sing, shout, proclaim, praise, and pray. Do you see that pray comes at the end of the actions? What makes prayer most effective is going through the previous stages.

So, let us be sure to enter into God's gates with thanksgiving and into His courts with praise. Specifically, we can give Him thanks and praise for what He is doing, and for what He is going to do for Israel.

Chapter 12
Confession of Sins

As we continue looking at the right approach to prayer, it is important to include a discussion on confession of sin.

A true intercessor is one who not only prays in a serious way, but also comes to confess sin before the Lord. The perfect example of this is Daniel, who was one of the most righteous men recorded in the Old Testament.

Identification

Though Daniel was an outstandingly righteous man, he identified himself with the sins of his people. If you are an intercessor, you cannot stand before God and say, "They have done wrong." That mindset doesn't get you anywhere with the Lord. You have to say, "We have done wrong."

It is imperative that you identify yourself with the sins of your family, your inheritance, your culture, your nation, or whatever situation you are praying for. In regard to Israel, Daniel says in chapter 9 verse 5:

> We have sinned...

Daniel does not say they have sinned, but he says we have sinned. Then he continues:

> ...and committed iniquity, we have done wickedly and rebelled, even by departing from Your precepts and Your judgments.

Is that true of Israel? It certainly is.

> Neither have we heeded Your servants the prophets, who spoke in Your name to our kings and our princes, to our fathers and all the people of the land. O LORD, righteousness belongs to You, but to us shame of face, as it is this day.
> O LORD, to us belongs shame of face, to our kings, our princes, and our fathers,

because we have sinned against You. To the LORD our God belong mercy and forgiveness, though we have rebelled against Him.

We could continue with that passage, but can you see the pattern? We can't be self-righteous.

We need to practice this principle of confessing the sins of the group we represent. We have got to stand in proxy just as Daniel did, because he was a righteous man. Yet he did not say of his fellow Jews, "They have sinned." He said, "We have sinned."

Personally, I believe it was Daniel's prayer that opened the way for the return of the Jews from Babylon to Israel. This example teaches us that confession is an essential part of effective intercession. We can be part of this activity of confession, but we should also be praying that God would release this act among both Gentiles and Jews.

Chapter 13
By God's Spirit

As we continue with this theme of taking the right approach to prayer, let us take a look now at the word of the Lord to Zerubbabel which is found in Zechariah 4:6:

> Not by might nor by power, but by My Spirit, says the LORD of hosts.

The "Lord of hosts" means the Lord of armies. God clearly understands might and power; He has it all. But He is saying that human might and power, laws and military power, will not accomplish what needs to be done. Those elements will not change the hearts of men and women. The only agent who can do that is the Holy Spirit.

We may tend to get upset about the political

situation in Israel, (and in our own nations, for that matter). But bear in mind that God is tolerating a lot of sin while He is waiting for His people. He doesn't approve of this sin, but He is tolerating it. The only power that will accomplish the transformations needed is the mysterious, invisible power of the Holy Spirit.

God is looking for a people whose hearts have been changed from hard stone to vibrant, responsive flesh. He will continue waiting until He has those kinds of people. There may be obstacles that prevent that process, but God says, "Too bad. I am waiting until I've got the people I am looking for." This transformation will only come by the Holy Spirit.

One of the greatest and most effective intercessory prayers is to pray for the release of the Holy Spirit upon Israel. It is beginning to happen, but there needs to be a great deal more.

Chapter 14
Mercy on Zion

Another directive for the right approach is to pray according to Psalm 102, verses 13 and 18. This is a revelation that was given to the psalmist in a mood of deep despair – He had come to the end of himself. He felt God had lifted him up and then thrown him away. What can be worse than that?

The opening verses of the psalm are all a mournful dirge. If you, like the psalmist, are struggling with depression (which is actually the most common psychological problem of Christians), you may want to do what the psalmist did. He looked away from his problems and looked to the Lord.

As long as you focus on your problems, you will have to live with them. In fact, if you focus too long your problems, you can start to believe there is no solution. Instead, we need to take in what the psalmist said in verse 12:

> But You, O LORD, shall endure forever, and the remembrance of Your name to all generations.

After he made this proclamation, the psalmist had a total change of mood.

Building up Zion

In the midst of this changed perspective, the psalmist had a revelation of the end time visitation of God upon the Jewish people:

> You will arise and have mercy on Zion: for the time to favor her, yes, the set time has come. For Your servants take pleasure in her stones, and show favor to her dust.

The next sections says:

> So the nations shall fear the name of the LORD, and all the kings of the earth Your

glory. For the LORD shall build up Zion; He shall appear in His glory.

God's intervention on behalf of Israel is destined to demonstrate His glory to the nations. In the old King James Version, this verse says, "When the LORD shall build up Zion, He shall appear in His glory." One of the great indications we are approaching the end of the age – and the Lord appearing in His glory – is that God is rebuilding Zion. Every one of us who love the Lord should be happy to witness the rebuilding of Zion. Let us continue to ask the Lord for mercy and favor as the set time approaches.

Chapter 15
The Set Time

A key factor for us in taking the right approach to prayer for Israel is the recognition of God's appointed times. In the passage we introduced in the previous chapter, Psalm 102, the psalmist said, "the time to favor her, yes, the set time has come." The Hebrew word for set time is *moed*. It is the word used of all the sacred festivals of Israel – Passover, Pentecost, Yom Kippur, the New Year – all of them.

One of the most effective forms of intercession is to say, "Lord, this is the set time to favor Zion. Please do what You have said."

Reminding the Lord

By way of illustration of this principle, I want to share a principle we have incorporated into the grace we have said at mealtimes since 1938, with some changes over the years.

The grace we say is simply a way of emphasizing the point we are making in this chapter: the right approach to prayer for Israel involves an awareness of His set time.

Dear Heavenly Father, bless our food in Jesus' name and the hands that prepared it. Show mercy and favor to Israel in this set time. Send revival to the United States, Great Britain, and the English-speaking world. Quicken our mortal bodies by your Holy Spirit and help us to eat wisely.

After that, we make a proclamation – for example 1 Thessalonians 5:23–24:

Now may the God of peace Himself sanctify us completely; and may our whole spirit, soul, and body be preserved blameless at the coming of the LORD Jesus Christ. He who calls us is faithful, who also will do it.

The reason I added the proclamation was to remind us of the effectiveness of praying for God to do what He said He will do at the set time.

Chapter 16
Avoiding Presumption

A final directive in the right approach to prayer involves an activity we need to avoid. When we pray, we must remove our presumptions. We must not tell God what to do.

Have you ever found yourself giving in to this tendency? If so, it will be helpful for us to turn to Isaiah 40 for a moment, starting with verse 13:

> Who has directed the Spirit of the LORD or as His counselor has taught Him? With whom did He take counsel, and who instructed Him, and taught Him in the path of justice? Who taught Him knowledge, and showed Him the way of understanding?

God is asking, "Do you think I need your advice? Do I need to be instructed by you?" This is a very common failing of Christians. They think God needs their advice – and they are prepared to tell Him what to do and how to do it.

Presumptuous Sin

May I give you a little advice from personal experience – from lessons that Ruth and I have learned the hard way. We have learned that without our realizing it, there can be a great deal of pride in our lives.

One of the Scriptures we were proclaiming was from Psalm 19: "Who can understand his errors? Cleanse me from secret faults." And God took us at our word. During that time, we took a sabbatical in Hawaii to seek God; He began to deal with us about our secret faults. One of the main facts God showed me out of Scripture was that the only way to have your sins forgiven is to confess them.

If we confess our sins, He is faithful and just to forgive us our sins and to cleanse us from all unrighteousness. (1 John 1:9)

If you don't confess your sins, God still loves you – but your sins are not forgiven. Ruth and I quickly discovered we had a lot of secret faults. The essence of most of them could be summed up in these words: presumptuous sins. What is one short, simple word for presumption? Pride. When we saw this truth, God required us to humble ourselves before Him and before one another.

This is my recipe for self-humbling: confess your sins to God. If you are married, confess them to your spouse. It is very hard to be arrogant with a wife or a husband to whom you have confessed your sins. I believe that this is an essential step for successful intercession.

The Barrier of Sin

We see a related principle in Isaiah 59, verses 1–2. These two verses in Isaiah which Gentile Christians always tend to believe are for the Jews. Actually, they apply to Jew and Gentile alike:

Behold, the LORD's hand is not shortened, that it cannot save; nor His ear heavy, that it cannot hear. But your iniquities have separated you from your God; and your sins have hidden His face from you, so that He will not hear.

The one supreme barrier to answered prayer is sin. Sin is not a respecter of nationalities or denominations. If we really want our prayers answered, we have to let God put His finger on our secret sins and then deal with them.

We have presumed on God. The Bible speaks about the need for the fear of the Lord about 250 times. That is the attitude we need which will keep us from being presumptuous.

As an exercise in the right approach to praying for Israel, let's humble ourselves, deal with our pride, and stop giving God advice. By taking these steps, we will avoid presumption and pray with the right attitude.

Section 4

Specific Prayers for Israel

Chapter 17

The Best Prayer for Israel

I n previous sections of this book, we have
discussed the people and the land of Israel,
culminating with the very important theme of
the right approach to praying for Israel. We will
now examine some specific themes for prayer as
revealed in Scripture.

"My Heart's Desire"

The best prayer you can pray is the one Paul
prayed in Romans 10 verse 1: "Brethren, my
heart's desire and prayer to God for Israel is
that they may be saved."

If a person is not saved, that person is lost.
There is no third option – nothing between the
two. The most important step in life for Jew or

Gentile is to be saved; to know that they are saved.

Personally, I have certain reservations about some people's excitement regarding what is going on in Israel and the restoration of the Jewish people to their land. Why do I say that? Because there are some Christians who think and act as though the only factor that matters is whether or not a person is Jewish. It is not!

Jesus said to the Jewish people in John 8:24, "If you do not believe that I am He [The Messiah], you will die in your sins." That is a Jew speaking to Jews.

There is no special salvation for Jews. There is no back door through which they can enter because they are Jewish. There is only one door for salvation – Jesus. In John 10:9, Jesus said, "I am the door. If anyone enters by Me, he will be saved."

So, if you are only going to pray one prayer for Israel, pray that they may be saved.

A Prerequisite

As we have already discussed, one of the prerequisites to Israel's salvation (and the return of

Jesus Christ) is for the Jews to be in their own land. Having established that all Israel needs to be saved, along with this requirement, we need to fulfil the next specific condition in order for the Lord to return. That prerequisite is the harvest of the Gentiles, which is confirmed in Romans 11:25:

> Blindness [or hardness] in part has happened to Israel until the fullness of the Gentiles has come in. And so all Israel will be saved.

All Israel will not be saved until every Gentile appointed by God for salvation has come into the kingdom. Therefore, if we are concerned about Israel, then we also have a very important reason to be concerned about the salvation of the Gentiles.

God's Ultimate Purpose

Our recognition that salvation of the Gentiles will usher in the harvest of the Jews helps us to understand God's heart in this matter. It helps us to identify with God's ultimate purpose for humanity.

So many times, we ask: why has God tolerated the appalling wickedness of humanity for hundreds and hundreds of years? What is He waiting for? My answer is: "He's waiting for a people for Himself."

That is what God is going to get out of history. Not an institution; not a lot of buildings; not a lot of government schemes. He is going to get a people for Himself.

I have been greatly moved on this subject by Titus 2:11–14:

> The grace of God that brings salvation has appeared to all men, teaching us that, denying ungodliness and worldly lusts, we should live soberly, righteously, and godly in the present age, looking for the blessed hope and glorious appearing of our great God and Savior Jesus Christ, who gave Himself for us, that He might redeem us from every lawless deed and purify for Himself His own special people, zealous for good works.

What does God intend to get out of history? "His own special people, zealous for good works." That is why He waits with endless patience while wickedness runs its course – because God has a chosen remnant, both Jew and Gentile. The Lord is not going to let history close until every one of them has come to Him through Jesus.

When you pray for Israel, don't start by praying for political issues. You can certainly do so if you like, but please realize that is not God's primary concern. What is primary is that Israel will become the special people God is after. The Lord is going to keep moving in this regard until He gets the special people He desires.

Chapter 18
Protection for Israel

Having lived for quite some time in Jerusalem, Ruth and I pray regularly for the protection of Israel. One of the prayers we voice is from Psalm 17:7–9, and we personalize this Scripture as we proclaim it.

> *Show Your marvellous lovingkindness by Your*
> *   right hand,*
> *O You who save those who trust in You*
> *From those who rise up against them.*
> *Keep [Israel] as the apple of Your eye;*
> *Hide [us] under the shadow of Your wings,*
> *From the wicked who oppress [us],*
> *From [our] deadly enemies who surround [us].*

The Scepter of the Wicked

There are two other passages in Psalms that provide an excellent foundation for prayer. The first passage is Psalm 125:3, which I am quoting from the NIV.

> The scepter of the wicked will not remain over the land allotted to the righteous.

What is "the scepter of the wicked"? I believe it is Islam. That being the case, Scripture says it will not remain over the land allotted to the righteous – nor will the power of Islam continue to dominate territory allotted to the righteous. In praying this scripture, it is important to recognize at the same time that the Lord is making the Jews righteous according to His plan. It is a double process, and we continually affirm this process with our prayers.

Those Who Hate Zion

Another scripture we proclaim is Psalm 129:5–6, which declares from the King James Version:

> Let them all be confounded and turned back that hate Zion. Let them be as the grass

upon the housetops, which withereth afore it groweth up.

Please take note here that the Lord is not talking in this verse about any nationality or denomination. The people to whom God is referring are "those who hate Zion." It doesn't matter whether they are professing Christians, Muslims, Buddhists, Hindus, or any other religion or nation. God is not against a nation; He is not against a denomination; He is not against a religion. However, He is against those who hate Zion. They will wither before Him. Their doom is sealed.

When you are praying, one of the best ways you can prepare yourself is to memorize Scriptures like those mentioned above. Rather than relying on the best prayer you can think of, these memorized Scriptures enable us to proclaim and pray for Israel with faith. Why is it so powerful? Because we know as we are praying and proclaiming that God desires to fulfill His Word.

Chapter 19
A Heart-Cry

To establish the next prayer theme regarding Israel, we need to ask ourselves the following question. "What is God waiting for?" As we have discussed previously, The Lord is waiting for a heart-cry from the Jewish people. We need to be praying that the Holy Spirit will cause a heart-cry to rise up from the Jewish people.

Our Gracious God

A wonderful insight on this principle is very clearly depicted in Isaiah 30, verses 18–19:

> Therefore the Lord will wait, that He may be gracious to you.

Please note that the reason the Lord is waiting is so He may be gracious to you. He may keep you waiting a long while, but eventually He will be gracious to you.

And therefore He will be exalted, that He may have mercy on you. For the Lord is a God of justice; blessed are all those who wait for Him. [Blessed are who? All those who wait for Him.] For the people shall dwell in Zion and Jerusalem [this is prophetic of the return of the Jews].

You shall weep no more. He will be very gracious to you at the sound of your cry; when He hears it, He will answer you.

God is waiting for the sound of the heart's cry of the Jewish people. That is why it is so important for us to pray that the Holy Spirit will put that cry into their heart.

Chapter 20
The Peace of Jerusalem

Continuing our discussion of specific prayers for Israel, there is another very obvious prayer with which you may be familiar. It is stated explicitly in Psalm 122, verse 6:

Pray for the peace of Jerusalem: "May they prosper who love you."

Some people consider the second sentence as part of the prayer. But I believe it is part of God's reward. When you love Jerusalem and pray for its peace, you will prosper.

God's Prophetic Purposes

It is important to note that when we pray for the peace of Jerusalem, we have to pray with an intelligent understanding of God's prophetic purposes. Such a prayer doesn't mean that peace will come down upon Jerusalem and everybody will stop fighting. Not at all. It means that we need to go on praying until God's purposes for the way peace will come to Jerusalem shall be worked out.

The truth of the matter is that Jerusalem will never know peace until the Prince of Peace comes. You may be living in Phoenix, Dubai, or Beijing, asking yourself, "Well, why should I pray for the peace of Jerusalem?" The answer to your question, as I understand it, is that God has arranged circumstances so that no other city on earth will know permanent peace until Jerusalem knows peace. When you pray for the peace of Jerusalem, you are also praying toward the peace of your own particular city in which you live.

The commandment of Psalm 122:6 is clear: we are to pray for the peace of Jerusalem.

Chapter 21

Bless – and Be Blessed!

The next recommendation I would offer for a specific prayer for Israel is expressed in this phrase: bless and be blessed. For an example that supports this premise, let's turn to Numbers 24 and the story of the prophet Balaam. He was a reluctant prophet who was hired by the heathen king, Balak, to curse Israel.

Balaam did his best to curse the Israelites, but under the overruling hand of God, he ended up blessing them more and more. Every time he tried harder to curse, he blessed instead. In verse 9, we find Balaam's final words. Speaking to Israel, he says:

Blessed is he who blesses you, and cursed is he who curses you.

God has given us a choice. We can either obtain a blessing or receive a curse. If you bless Israel, God will bless you. But if you curse Israel, God will curse you.

You Can Choose

In my book called *Blessing or Curse, You Can Choose*, the first theme I deal with is determining if you are under a blessing or a curse. The next theme covered is how to get out from under the curse and get into the blessing. In the encouragement I offer for that theme, I deal with most of the common causes for curses. One of the commonest and the most destructive is anti-Semitism, which can bring the curse of God upon an individual, a community, a church, a nation, or a civilization. In that regard, I relate the testimony of a Palestinian Arab who is a personal friend of mine.

When he migrated to the United States and went into business, he became very successful. Then he went bankrupt. In the course of that experience, he met the Lord and received the Holy Spirit. Immediately God began to deal with him – not only about his finances, but also about his anti-Semitism. Eventually he realized that because of his Arab background he had always held resentment against the Jews – even to the point of cursing them. He realized that this practice carried with it a curse upon him and his family.

One day, in the presence of the Lord, he said, "I renounce any resentment in my heart toward the Jewish people. I forgive them." Immediately something changed inside of him. He realized that his finances had not been under a blessing but under a curse – a curse of insufficiency.

When he was released from the curse of anti-Semitism (and the curse of insufficiency that went with it), his income began to increase so he could give liberally to the work of the Kingdom of God. His is a wonderful testimony which illustrates so clearly that it does not pay to curse the Jews. It doesn't pay to have resentment in your heart against them. If we want to be blessed, then we have to bless Israel. Blessing Israel, in a sense, is simply enlightened self-interest.

As we pray, we have a wonderful opportunity

to bless the Jewish people. Blessing them in this way enables God to bless us. In touching upon specific prayers for Israel, I want you to remember that blessing Israel is something which not only blesses them as a nation; it also returns blessings on you as well.

Chapter 22
Proclaim!

As you step by faith into this practice of praying specific prayers for Israel, I want to strongly encourage you to take up the sword of the Spirit. Proclaim! It is one of the most powerful actions you can take on behalf of Israel.

We have touched upon the use of proclamation in previous chapters, discussing its power when praying for the protection of Israel. However, proclamation is not limited to this area. In this chapter, I want to show you how to pray God's Word into effect.

Specific Proclamations

In the section that follows, I would like to give

you a pattern of proclamations on behalf of Israel that Ruth and I regularly declare.

The first one is taken from Psalm 33, verses 8–12:

> Let all the earth fear the LORD, let all the inhabitants of the world stand in awe of Him. For He spoke, and it was done; He commanded, and it stood fast. The LORD brings the counsel of the nations to nothing; He makes the plans of the peoples of no effect.
>
> The counsel of the LORD stands forever, the plans of His heart to all generations. Blessed is the nation whose God is the LORD, the people He has chosen as His own inheritance.

The name of that people is Israel. Everything the nations plan which is contrary to God's plans for Israel will not come to pass.

In Jeremiah 31:10, a part of the verse says:

> He who scattered Israel will gather him, and keep him as a shepherd does his flock.

Please take time to read this passage again. It is short, but powerful. Regathered Israel is ultimately secure – not merely because God has brought them together, but because He has promised also to keep them.

When you combine these Scriptures with the others which are mentioned throughout this book, you have a list of proclamations you can make. However, it is not meant to be a definitive or comprehensive list of proclamations on behalf of Israel. You may discover others.

If there is a situation regarding Israel which you want to pray about, ask the Lord to show you the relevant Scriptures to proclaim. There is simply no limit to the power God will release through this practice of proclaiming!

Chapter 23
God's Heart for Israel

In the past few chapters, we have talked about making specific prayers and proclamations on behalf of Israel. But are we truly prepared to do so?

There may be a prior step we need to take to prepare our hearts through confession and brokenness to enter into this life-changing, monumental work.

Are You Willing?

I want to ask you a question in this moment: Are you willing to ask Jesus to give you His heart for the Jewish people? Are you willing to enter into an identification with the appalling evil that has been done in the name of Christ to the Jewish people? Are you willing to confess and repent for the continuing prejudices that are like an inundating tide?

You see, there has to occur some kind of a breakthrough – some kind of brokenness. Basically, most Christians and most of the Church are standing with folded arms contemplating the scene. We are too stiff, too shut up, too afraid to let our feelings be seen. We are too afraid to enter into the feelings of Jesus for the situation. You and I cannot be intercessors in any real sense until we share the burden of the Lord for the situation for which we are praying.

At this point in our study, I am suggesting that we should put all we have learned into practice by dealing deeper with indifference, confession, and the seeking of forgiveness.

We simply need to humble ourselves before God and say, "God, we have sinned. We have been guilty of the blood of the Jewish people. We, the Christian Church collectively, for sixteen centuries have been the main instigators and perpetrators of anti-Semitism." Here is a prayer to help you to start the process:

"Lord Jesus Christ, You who are head over all things to the Church which is Your Body. We stand before You, Lord, and acknowledge with shame and sorrow our unutterable guilt in the sufferings of the Jewish people. O God, there is no way that we can express the sense of guilt and sorrow that has come upon us.

Now we stand before You, not merely to acknowledge our own personal sins, but we stand before You on behalf of the sins of the Christian church. We are not indicating any particular denomination or section of the Church. We are repenting on behalf of the whole Church.

We are ashamed before You of our indifferences, Lord. O God, we are ashamed of my hardness and of our materialism. We have let so many obstacles come between us and the interests of Your kingdom and the purposes of Your heart.

Forgive us, Lord. Blot out our sins as a cloud, and our transgressions as a thick cloud. Blot them out because of Your mercy, Lord. Blot out the dark cloud that hangs over the

Church in this land because of anti-Semitism, Lord – that dark cloud which withholds the real outpouring of Your blessing. Blot it out, Lord, we pray, in Jesus' name.

We ask again that You would pour out upon us, Lord, a spirit of grace and of supplications. Release Your Spirit upon us in Jesus' name. Amen."

You may also consider if you are not Jewish, that you might be given some opportunity to express your sorrow and repentance toward the Jewish people. As you continue to pray, open your heart to the Lord. Pray that God would give you His heart for His people, Israel.

Don't rush. Wait on God, and pray until you have received a breakthrough.

Section 6

A Higher Level

Chapter 24
A Higher Vision

As we come to the end of this message, I want to close with what I call "My Vision." Admittedly, this is very subjective, but I want to share it with you in the hope that it may speak to your heart.

When I was living in Jerusalem, I would meet early every Friday morning to pray with a group of men. Most of these men were Jewish – some were not. We were deeply concerned about the political developments in Israel. Often we would ask the Lord, "Please don't let the government do this," or "don't let the government do that." After a while, I realized that what we were doing was praying out of reaction. The initiative belonged to somebody else, and we were just responding.

SECTION 6

The Breaker-Through

As I was considering this posture of reacting, I said to myself, "I don't believe that is all that God does. God doesn't merely react. God initiates." When I began to seek God for what He would do, a verse from Micah 2:13 came to me. It said, "The one that breaketh-through is gone up before them... the king passeth on before them." (Darby Bible Translation) I thought, "That's right. God is the breaker-through. He moves on a higher level than politics. And when He breaks through, there is truly a breakthrough."

As I continued to ponder this idea, it raised the next question, "What is the higher level on which God will break through?" In response to this question, I sensed the Lord giving me this answer: prayer, intercession, and spiritual warfare.

A Higher Realm

In that realm of prayer, intercession, and spiritual warfare, we move in a higher level than anything that politics, leaders, or even dictators can do.

That higher realm is where the victory lies. We don't have to sit passively, wringing our hands and saying, "Oh dear, what next?" Jesus wants us to take the initiative – but it has to originate with Him. He is the head of the Church. All initiative comes from Him.

As I was thinking about the debt of Gentile Christians to the Jewish people, this thought came to me: the way we really can begin to repay our debt is by giving ourselves systematically to intercession for Israel, their land, and their destiny.

I am not a person who has many visions. But I want to challenge you to ask yourself, "Is God calling me, or calling the group I am in, to prayer warfare for Israel?"

That prayer warfare is the plane on which we will win the battle. We will not win it with political moves. We will not win it with finances. We will not win through armaments. Rather we can operate on a plane higher than any the enemy can ever attain to – the plane of intercession.

An Invitation

As you have read this book, has something stirred in your heart concerning the Jewish people and the land of Israel? As you have grown in your understanding of the Biblical mandate to pray for Israel, do you want to do more? Have you understood, perhaps for the first time, the unfathomable debt we owe to the Jewish people?

If your answer to those questions is a resounding, "Yes," I want to invite you to pray the following prayer with me. By doing so, we will be asking God to help us be the people He has called us to be – the ones who will intercede for Israel and the Jewish people. By doing so, we will be paving the way for the return of Christ – able to say, along with the Apostle John, "Amen. Even so, come Lord Jesus." (Revelation 22:20)

> Father, I want to start by saying, "Thank you!" Thank you for Israel, both the land and the people. Thank You that You have chosen the land for Your people and that You will uphold Your Word against all odds.
>
> Thank You for Your salvation which comes to me through the death, burial, and resurrection of our Savior, Yeshua Messiah, who was born to a Jewish mother in Bethlehem, Israel.
>
> Thank You for bringing to our attention

the persecution the Jewish people have experienced through the ages. Please help us not to forget it simply because it is unpleasant, but please use it to spur us on to prayer, intercession, and practical help for Your people, Israel.

We praise You for the way You are regathering Israel to the land You gave them by covenant. To You alone be the glory for the restoration of Your people and the softening of their hearts taking place now.

With this prayer, we now submit ourselves to You completely for Your purposes and Your will to be done in and through us. Teach us, remind us, and quicken us to intercede for Israel. As we pray, remind us of the words Paul spoke in Romans 11:12: "If their [Jews] fall is riches for the world, and their failure riches for the Gentiles, how much more their fullness!" Please bring them to that point of restoration and fullness we pray, in Yeshua's name. Amen.

About the Author

DEREK PRINCE (1915–2003) was born in India of British parents. Educated as a scholar of Greek and Latin at Eton College and Cambridge University, England, he held a Fellowship in Ancient and Modern Philosophy at King's College. He also studied several modern languages, including Hebrew and Aramaic, at Cambridge University and the Hebrew University in Jerusalem.

While serving with the British army in World War II, he began to study the Bible and experienced a life-changing encounter with Jesus Christ. Out of this encounter he formed two conclusions: first, that Jesus Christ is alive; second, that the Bible is a true, relevant, up-to-date book.

These conclusions altered the whole course of his life, which he then devoted to studying and teaching the Bible.

Derek's main gift of explaining the Bible and its teaching in a clear and simple way has helped build a foundation of faith in millions of lives. His non-denominational, non-sectarian approach has made his teaching equally relevant and helpful to people from all racial and religious backgrounds.

He is the author of over 50 books, 600 audio and 100 video teachings, many of which have been translated and published in more than 100 languages. His daily radio broadcast is translated into Arabic, Chinese (Amoy, Cantonese, Mandarin, Shanghainese, Swatow), Croatian, German, Malagasy, Mongolian, Russian, Samoan, Spanish and Tongan. The radio program continues to touch lives around the world.

Derek Prince Ministries continues to reach out to believers in over 140 countries with Derek's teachings, fulfilling the mandate to keep on "until Jesus returns". This is effected through the outreaches of more than 30 Derek Prince

ABOUT THE AUTHOR

Offices around the world, including primary work in Australia, Canada, China, France, Germany, the Netherlands, New Zealand, Norway, Russia, South Africa, Switzerland, the United Kingdom and the United States. For current information about these and other worldwide locations, visit www.derekprince.com

Books by Derek Prince

Appointment in Jerusalem
At the End of Time*
Authority and Power of God's Word*
Be Perfect
Blessing or Curse: You Can Choose
Bought with Blood
By Grace Alone
Called to Conquer
Choice of a Partner, The
Complete Salvation
Declaring God's Word
Derek Prince – A Biography
by Stephen Mansfield
Derek Prince: On Experiencing God's Power
Destiny of Israel and The Church, The

Divine Exchange, The
Doctrine of Baptisms, The*
Does Your Tongue Need Healing?
Entering the Presence of God
Expelling Demons
Explaining Blessings and Curses
Extravagant Love
Faith and Works*
Faith to Live By
Fasting
Final Judgment*
First Mile, The
Foundational Truths for Christian Living
Founded on the Rock*
Gifts of the Spirit, The
God is a Matchmaker
God's Medicine Bottle
God's Plan for Your Money
God's Remedy for Rejection
God's Will for Your Life
God's Word Heals
Grace of Yielding, The
Harvest Just Ahead, The
Holy Spirit in You, The

How to Fast Successfully
Husbands and Fathers
Immersion in The Spirit*
Judging
Key to the Middle East, The
Keys to Successful Living
Laying the Foundations Series*
Life's Bitter Pool
Life-Changing Spiritual Power
Living as Salt and Light
Lucifer Exposed
Marriage Covenant, The
Orphans, Widows, the Poor and Oppressed
Our Debt to Israel
Pages from My Life's Book
Partners for Life
Philosophy, the Bible and the Supernatural
Power in the Name
Power of the Sacrifice, The
Prayers and Proclamations
Praying for the Government
Promise of Provision, The
Prophetic Guide to the End Times
Protection from Deception

Will You Intercede?
You Matter to God
You Shall Receive Power

Get the Complete Laying the Foundations Series*

1. Founded on the Rock (B100)
2. Authority and Power of God's Word (B101)
3. Through Repentance to Faith (B102)
4. Faith and Works (B103)
5. The Doctrine of Baptisms (B104)
6. Immersion in The Spirit (B105)
7. Transmitting God's Power (B106)
8. At the End of Time (B107)
9. Resurrection of the Body (B108)
10. Final Judgment (B109)

Derek Prince Ministries
www.derekprince.com

Derek Prince Ministries Offices Worldwide

DPM – Asia/Pacific
38 Hawdon Street
Sydenham
Christchurch 8023
New Zealand
T: + 64 3 366 4443
E: admin@dpm.co.nz
W: www.dpm.co.nz and www.derekprince.in

DPM – Australia
15 Park Road
Seven Hills
New South Wales 2147

Australia
T: +61 2 9838 7778
E: enquiries@au.derekprince.com
W: www.derekprince.com.au

DPM – Canada
P.O. Box 8354 Halifax
Nova Scotia B3K 5M1
Canada
T: + 1 902 443 9577
E: enquiries.dpm@eastlink.ca
W: www.derekprince.org

DPM – France
B.P. 31, Route d'Oupia
34210 Olonzac
France
T: + 33 468 913872
E: info@derekprince.fr
W: www.derekprince.fr

DPM – Germany
Söldenhofstr. 10
83308 Trostberg
Germany

T: + 49 8621 64146
E: ibl@ibl-dpm.net
W: www.ibl-dpm.net

DPM – Netherlands
Nobelstraat 7–08
7131 PZ Lichtenvoorde
Netherlands
T: +31 251–255044
E: info@derekprince.nl
W: www.derekprince.nl

DPM – Norway
P.O. Box 129
Lodderfjord
N-5881 Bergen
Norway
T: +47 928 39855
E: sverre@derekprince.no
W: www.derekprince.no

Derek Prince Publications Pte. Ltd.
P.O. Box 2046
Robinson Road Post Office
Singapore 904046

T: + 65 6392 1812
E: dpmchina@singnet.com.sg
W: www.dpmchina.org (English)
www.ygmweb.org (Chinese)

DPM – South Africa
P.O. Box 33367
Glenstantia
0010 Pretoria
South Africa
T: +27 12 348 9537
E: enquiries@derekprince.co.za
W: www.derekprince.co.za

DPM – Switzerland
Alpenblick 8
CH-8934 Knonau
Switzerland
T: + 41 44 768 25 06
E: dpm-ch@ibl-dpm.net
W: www.ibl-dpm.net

DPM – UK
PO Box 393
Hitchin SG5 9EU

United Kingdom
T: + 44 1462 492100
E: enquiries@dpmuk.org
W: www.dpmuk.org

DPM – USA
P.O. Box 19501
Charlotte NC 28219
USA
T: + 1 704 357 3556
E: ContactUs@derekprince.org
W: www.derekprince.org

CPSIA information can be obtained
at www.ICGtesting.com
Printed in the USA
BVHW080724170720
583830BV00006B/699